WALKING
IN THE REALM

OF THE

MIRACULOUS

LOVE—THE ULTIMATE PLAN
OF GOD'S POWER

KENNETH COPELAND

KENNETH COPELAND
PUBLICATIONS

All scripture is from the *King James Version* of the Bible.

Walking in the Realm of the Miraculous

Love—The Ultimate Plan of God's Power

Previously published as The Miraculous Realm of God's Love

ISBN-10 0-88114-784-2   30-0032

ISBN-13 978-0-88114-784-1

25 24 23 22 21 20   19 18 17 16 15 14

Kenneth Copeland Publications

Fort Worth, TX 76192-0001

For more information about Kenneth Copeland Ministries, visit kcm.org or call
1-800-600-7395 (U.S. only) or +1-817-852-6000.

Contents

Walking in the Realm of the Miraculous:
Love—The Ultimate Plan of God's Power

A PROPHECY

Dr. Kenneth E. Hagin, a powerful man of God, gave forth a prophetic message in a service held in Houston, Texas in 1979.

That message burned into my consciousness. The inspiration of that message brought about the writing of this book. I want to share that message with you.

Read it several times. It will not only thrill you, it will cause great determination to rise within you to become one of the "new breed."

The end is not yet. Yes, the Lord cometh. But in these days there is coming a mighty move of the Spirit of God. You are only in the edge of it. You've touched the realm of the miraculous. Every believer has touched the realm of the miraculous.

You touched the realm of the miraculous when you were born again. Your spirit, your inward man, your inner man, became a new man instantly in Christ Jesus—a new creature— old things passed away and all things became new; you touched the miraculous and that's as far as some have ever gone.

Others have entered into the holy pages of the Holy Writ of the Father God. They've seen that they could be empowered with the Spirit from on high. They entered into a further realm of the miraculous and were filled with the Holy Ghost and began to speak with a new tongue and in a heavenly language.

Yea, their hearts did thrill and their spirits were glad, but ere the cares of life crept in. Instead of staying in the Word and renewing their minds with the Word and staying, as the Scriptures instruct, "filled with the Spirit," they only touched the realm of the miraculous.

Occasionally in prayer, occasionally in the hour of great need—of emergency—they would enter into that realm. The Spirit of God would minister unto them and sometimes minister through them. Then they would slip back into the natural.

But some renewed their minds with the Word. They began to see that the gifts and manifestations of the Spirit were for them. They dedicated themselves and consecrated themselves and separated themselves from the carnal, from the natural, so that they could be holy vessels meet for the Master's use. They stepped further into the realm of the miraculous.

There has been and there is now a revival—a reviving—a renewal as some would call it; a move down through the years. In these days, the manifestation of the Spirit—the power of God in manifestation—has touched all people of all churches, but the end is not yet. For you've only stepped into the waters that the prophet of the Old Testament prophesied about. You've only stepped in knee deep. He prophesied that they would walk out until the waters would be up to their loins, and walk on out even further; water being a type of the Spirit of God.

Not only in these days will all of the gifts that have been in manifestation to some extent be in further manifestation, but the ministry gifts also will be in manifestation. Men will stand in the office of the prophet in the full measure, not just in the partial measure—as I have, as some have—but in the full measure. And men shall rejoice.

At the same time evil men and seducers shall wax worse and worse. Those that are deceived and desire not the truth but rather love darkness shall become darker still. Many will look into the world and say, "Satan and his works are abounding." Their eyes will be closed to what God is doing. But He will prepare for Himself a Body. Yea, a Body of believers who will rise up strong in faith. They will be strong and do exploits.

He is raising up and will raise up what those in the natural vernacular would call a "new breed." They'll not be inhibited by the traditions of the past, nor shall they be downcast because of the negativism of the past, nor shall they be circumscribed and hindered and held in because of the thinking of men. But knowing their rights and privileges in Christ, they shall rise up with the Name of the Lord Jesus Christ, and it shall be said of them as it was of those in the New Testament: "They that have turned the world upside down are come hither also."

So prepare ye the way of the Lord, for the Lord cometh. But occupy until He comes!

MESSAGE FROM KENNETH COPELAND

As believers we have just passed over a spiritual threshold, embarking on the greatest outpouring of the Spirit of God that has ever been on the face of the earth. We are dealing with a worldwide sweeping of television by the power of God. We are dealing with the greatest mass sweeping of souls into the kingdom of God that has ever been exercised by the Holy Spirit.

God has built an army of believers and it is already in operation. This army continues to grow as new converts are brought in, and we are not in the training stages any longer. Thank God, we are on the move! God's expeditionary forces are in the field, and we are part of it.

In recent years, there has come a great wave of revelation knowledge concerning the new birth. There was a time when people thought Dwight L. Moody was a heretic for what he preached from the Word of God. They could not understand how any man could say that God loved the sinner. Today, we know without a doubt that God's love is for every person on earth. We have seen the truth of John 3:16, *"For God so loved the world, that he gave his only begotten Son."*

Since those early days, there have been great moves of God. We have watched a great healing revival. During the 1960s, God caused a great revelation of the Holy Spirit to flow through the Body of Christ. Everyone began discussing and experiencing the Baptism in the Holy Spirit.

This great move of God today involves two particular areas about which there has been very little revelation knowledge. One is the realm of prosperity. There is a wider scope to prosperity than just financial matters and having your own personal needs met. The world measures prosperity in silver and gold, but God's prosperity is not based on a monetary system. True prosperity is the ability to use the power of God to meet the needs of mankind. Of course, this includes finances, but it also includes all the things money can't buy—things such as healing, peace of mind, answers to social and political problems, etc. All these are a part of the revival occurring today in the earth.

The second area involves a revelation of the love of God. The Lord said to me a number of years ago: "A revelation of the love of God is the highest revelation of the Church because I am love." To have a revelation of the love of God is to have a revelation—not of what He has or what He can do—but of God Himself. God is love, and He is revealing His love as never before to the world today. I believe with all my heart that it is the revelation of God's love in the Body of Christ that will usher in the Great Resurrection.

On March 23, 1979, the Lord spoke to me about broadcasting the truth of God's love through every available avenue. At that time, I received the commission to do it. I said, "I receive the commission from God to establish a place so filled with love that it will overwhelm everyone who comes in contact with it—a place where love is king! I am to put this love on radio and television to the nations until it causes revival everywhere. It will bring peace between labor and management, men and their wives, churches, even governments. I will work tirelessly to fulfill this commission."

The Lord said to me: "I want you to preach and tell people that My mercy endureth forever. Teach them and tell them how to walk in the love walk. Train them and let them realize that My love is alive, that My love is powerful, that faith worketh by love, that in love there is no occasion to stumbling, that they can walk in My love and be perfected in it before they come to heaven, that My love will protect them. I want them to know the reality of My Word that says, *'Above all things, have a fervent love for one another.'"* The Greek text of I Peter 4:8 says, *"Above all things, have a white-hot love for one another."* The Bible says we are baptized with the Holy Ghost and with fire (Luke 3:16). That fire is the all-consuming love of God. God's love will consume sin. It will consume death. It will consume the work of Satan and absolutely swallow it up.

In the past, God's people had to be backed against a wall with no way to go before they would reach out to touch the miraculous. Today, there is a vast army of men and women who have made the decision to live and walk in the realm of the miraculous. The love of God is the key to walking in that realm. There are things available to us in walking in the love of God that are not available any other way. Every problem that has ever defeated anyone in the Body of Christ was a result of not walking in the love of God. God, His Word, His Spirit and His Name work well in every situation. They are successful in all realms.

In this day and hour, we as God's people are taking our rightful position, dedicating ourselves to God, renewing our minds with the Word, setting ourselves apart from the carnal ways of the world and committing ourselves to walk in the love of God. Surrounded by His love, we are now walking in the realm of the miraculous.

Kenneth Copeland

Faith in God's Love

When you receive a revelation of the love of God, you will have insight into something that does not fail. Think about that. In this world where nothing is failure proof, we have been given complete access to God's love. Love is the cardinal law of God—and it never fails. Put the love of God into operation and you will succeed (1 Corinthians 13:8).

It is a must that you learn how to operate in God's love. To do that requires faith. You have to develop your faith in His love to the point that it governs your thinking, your speech and your actions. You must have your mind so renewed that you function entirely according to God's love rather than the methods and systems of the world.

The world's systems and ideas are accepted as the norm, but they are not the norm. God's Word is the norm and the standard of life we are to maintain. Man was created to function on God's level. Adam walked on that level in the Garden of Eden; but when he disobeyed God, he fell from his position of fellowship and oneness with God. It took Jesus coming to earth as a man to reclaim the authority Adam gave over to Satan. Today, every born-again believer can live on that supernatural level through the power of the Holy Spirit. John 16:13 says the Holy Spirit was sent to lead and guide us into all truth.

As a born-again believer, you have the same spiritual capacity Jesus has. If you spend time studying and meditating on God's Word and living in the Word the way Jesus did, then you can have every ounce of faith, wisdom and understanding operating in you that Jesus had during His earthly ministry. It is available to you because the Holy Spirit is available to you.

Not only do you have the same capacity for faith as Jesus, you also have the same capacity for love. This can be proven very easily through God's Word. Romans 5:5 says, "...*the love of God is shed abroad in our hearts by the Holy Ghost which is given unto us.*" Jesus said to the Father while praying, "*And I have declared unto them thy name, and will declare it: that the love wherewith thou has loved me may be in them, and I in them"* (John 17:26). Notice He said the same love, with which the Father loves Him, is in us! That is hard to accept, but you know Jesus didn't pray something that wasn't true, nor did He pray something that wasn't answered. You have the very love of God, Himself, in your heart—not just part of it, *all* of it. Praise God! You need to allow a revelation of that truth to grow in your consciousness to the place where you fully realize God Almighty lives in you! This truth has never been fully received in the Body of Christ. Through religious traditions, we have belittled ourselves by not knowing who we are in Christ Jesus and not understanding the fullness of God that is in us through Him. Ignorance has robbed us of God's best and kept us below the standard of life God desires for us to have.

Your spirit is just as big as God's because you are born of Him. My son has the same capacity for strength that I have. He has just as many muscles in his body as I have in mine; but at his present age he is not as strong as I am. Why? Because his muscles are not fully developed. He is still growing. He has all the physical components of a full-grown man—bones, muscles, organs, etc.—but he is not yet a man. How his muscles develop depends on how he treats his body. He can nourish it properly or he can destroy it. He can build it up or tear it down. He is a human being with the right and privilege to choose his own way.

There are two factors involved here: capacity and choice.

There is no way to have one without the other. However, with the choice comes the responsibility. You are responsible for what you do with and to your physical body. In the same way, you are responsible for your spirit. When you were born again your spirit was completely made new—with great capacity for faith and hope and love. If you waste your spirit, you will pay the consequences.

"His Mercy Endureth Forever"

Then shall the trees of the wood sing out at the presence of the Lord, because he cometh to judge the earth. O give thanks unto the Lord; for he is good; for his mercy endureth for ever (1 Chronicles 16:33-34).

The word *mercy* is the same word translated "compassion" and "love." Many times the translators of the New Testament used the word "charity." They were trying to convey the giving aspect of love. It is not possessive and selfish; it is a giver.

It came even to pass, as the trumpeters and singers were as one, to make one sound to be heard in praising and thanking the Lord; and when they lifted up their voice with the trumpets and cymbals and instruments of musick, and praised the Lord, saying, For he

is good; for his mercy endureth for ever: that then the
house was filled with a cloud, even the house of the
Lord; so that the priests could not stand to minister
by reason of the cloud: for the glory of the Lord had
filled the house of God (2 Chronicles 5:13-14).

When you talk about love moving, you are talking
about God moving. God is love! (1 John 4:8). His mercy
endureth forever!

Let's look at 2 Chronicles 7:1-3:

Now when Solomon had made an end of praying, the
fire came down from heaven, and consumed the burnt
offering and the sacrifices; and the glory of the Lord
filled the house. And the priests could not enter into
the house of the Lord, because the glory of the Lord
had filled the Lord's house. And when all the children
of Israel saw how the fire came down, and the glory of
the Lord upon the house, they bowed themselves with
their faces to the ground upon the pavement, and
worshipped, and praised the Lord, saying, For he is
good; for his mercy endureth for ever.

Now look at Chapter 20:20-21:

And they rose early in the morning, and went forth
into the wilderness of Tekoa: and as they went forth,
Jehoshaphat stood and said, Hear me, O Judah, and
ye inhabitants of Jerusalem; Believe in the Lord your
God, so shall ye be established; believe his prophets,
so shall ye prosper. And when he had consulted with
the people, he appointed singers unto the Lord, and
that should praise the beauty of holiness, as they went
out before the army, and to say, Praise the Lord; for
his mercy endureth for ever.

Enemy armies had invaded Israel and Jehoshaphat pro-
claimed to the people that he would send out praisers to go
before the army. Put yourself in that situation. How would
you react if you had been picked as one of the praisers? You
were going to go out ahead of your army and face a few
thousand enemy soldiers! That was quite an assignment.

And when they began to sing and to praise, the Lord
set ambushments against the children of Ammon,
Moab, and mount Seir, which were come against
Judah; and they were smitten. For the children of
Ammon and Moab stood up against the inhabitants of
mount Seir, utterly to slay and destroy them: and
when they had made an end of the inhabitants of Seir,

every one helped to destroy another. And when Judah
came toward the watch tower in the wilderness, they
looked unto the multitude, and, behold, they were
dead bodies fallen to the earth, and none escaped
(2 Chronicles 20:22-24).

God moved when those people operated in the love of
God rather than in the power of military might. The result
was total defeat of the enemy:

And when Jehoshaphat and his people came to take
away the spoil of them, they found among them in
abundance both riches with the dead bodies, and precious jewels, which they stripped off for themselves,
more than they could carry away: and they were three
days in gathering of the spoil, it was so much
(2 Chronicles 20:25).

These were armies—trained troops. God didn't send His
power to kill those people. They made a choice—they did it
to themselves. They could have gone to Israel and said, "We
bring offerings unto the Most High God. We bring our jewels and our goods. We want to join with you. We want to
serve God with you." Israel would have answered, "Come
on in and let's worship and praise the Most High God, for

If you don't choose the path of love, then Satan will try to take advantage of you at every turn.

His mercy endureth forever."

Those singers and praisers were obeying God and giving witness to God's love and mercy. This is a beautiful illustration of faith in the love of God. However, we must remember this: To fight against love is to fight against God; and God (love) never fails. So who will fail?

You have a choice. If you don't choose the path of love, then Satan will try to take advantage of you at every turn. He will come against you every chance he gets.

God's love sent Jesus to the cross for us. We were not worthy, but God did it anyway! His mercy endures forever! Hallelujah!

Faith Works by Love

For an in-depth study of the love of God, the place to start is 1 John. John is called the apostle of love. In the first chapter he explained why he wrote it: So we could fellowship together with God the Father and with His Son Jesus Christ. *Without a revelation of the love of God, you will never have close fellowship and communion with Him.* There will always be an unwarranted fear of God if you don't know God loves you.

Let's look at 1 John 4:15-16. *"Whosoever shall confess that*

Jesus is the Son of God, God dwelleth in him and he in God. And we have known and believed the love that God hath to us. God is love; and he that dwelleth in love dwelleth in God, and God in him." Here is the answer to the prayer Jesus prayed in John 17. He prayed that the love the Father had for Him would be in us. *"...that the love wherewith thou has loved me may be in them, and I in them"* (John 17:26). God is love and love is God, so he that dwells in love dwells in God and God in him.

The following is a prophetic utterance given during one of our meetings as we were studying the love of God.

Remove from your thinking, saith God, *that love is a form of nothing. Love is not a form of nothing or just a state of mind. Love is a reality. I am love.*

When you are talking about love, saith the Lord, *you are not talking about a feeling. You are not talking about something that is a state. You are talking about a living being. You are talking about Me. When you speak of love,* saith the Spirit of Grace, *you are speaking about all that I am, all that I can do, all I ever was, and all I ever shall be.*

One day the Spirit of God said to me, *You don't understand My motive when I said to turn the other cheek. If you will retaliate in My love by faith, instead of retaliating in the arm of the flesh, you can develop My power and My love in you until they are perfected and I will keep you protected all the time.*

When Jesus said, "Turn the other cheek," He didn't intend for you to get beaten up. He intended for you to be walking in the love of God so powerfully that when you do turn your other cheek, the enemy can't hit you! Look at 1 John 5:18, *"...he that is begotten of God [love] keepeth himself,* **and that wicked one toucheth him not."** That is the greatest testimony of love in the physical realm. God has never asked us to be a lamb to the slaughter. Jesus was the Lamb of God. He was slaughtered in our place.

By misunderstanding His motive, we have just laid our heads on the block and let the devil cut them off. The Word does not say subordinate yourself to Satan. It says, *"Resist the devil, and he will flee from you"* (James 4:7). But our ideas of resistance have been centered in the natural, physical realm. We are not in a physical combat with Satan. He is a spirit being; we must fight him with spiritual weapons. *"The weapons of our warfare are not carnal, but mighty through God to the pulling down of strong holds"* (2 Corinthians 10:4). These strongholds are not human. We don't wrestle with flesh and blood, but with principalities and powers, and rulers of the darkness of this world and wicked spirits in heavenly places (Ephesians 6:12). Once you stop Satan's operation, you won't have any trouble with people doing you harm.

A graphic illustration of this is Jesus' reaction to the murder of John the Baptist. You have to remember that John and Jesus were related. In the natural realm, they were cousins, but their kinship went deeper than that. John was the only man at that time who knew Jesus was the Messiah. He was the only man who walked in the power of the Holy Spirit and in the office of prophet while Jesus was on earth. There was a ministerial kinship between them.

Then John was brutally murdered. When Jesus heard of John's death, He went off to a desert place to be alone, but the people followed Him. They made a demand on His ability. *"And Jesus went forth, and saw a great multitude, and was moved with compassion toward them, and he healed their sick"* (Matthew 14:14). When He saw them, He was moved with compassion—not a feeling of compassion, but Compassion, Himself.

Compassion said, *"Go ye into all the world, and preach the gospel to every creature."* Compassion said, *"Lay hands on the sick, and they shall recover."* Compassion told Jesus to heal the sick and save the lost.

Compassion was manifest as Jesus laid hands on the sick in that desert place. Herod wasn't Jesus' enemy, Satan was. Jesus retaliated for the murder of John—not in the natural, but in the spirit. He didn't fight Herod with His fists. He reacted in the realm of the spirit, in the realm of faith and love. He attacked His real enemy, which was Satan, by healing the sick!

To understand these things, you need to understand God's motive. He does not intend for us to be the world's whipping boys. We were not made to be spiritual rugs for

Satan to wipe his feet on. His desire is to put us in a place where we will never fail. How would you like to operate in a zero failure rate? You can. There is one way: through love. The Bible says love never fails.

Let's look again at I John 5:18. *"We know that whosoever is born of God sinneth not."* This does not mean that if you sin you are not born of God. It means you are not a practicer of sin, you are not looking for a way to sin, but you are doing your best to keep out of it. Whosoever is born of love sinneth not. A step out of love is a step into sin.

The second part of that verse says, *"...but he that is begotten of God keepeth himself, and that wicked one toucheth him not."* The man who is born of God is born of love. When he is walking the love walk, he can laugh in Satan's face. Satan cannot harm you when you are walking in love.

God has a spiritual capsule, and this capsule goes into effect when you get into the Word and allow God to minister to you. God will, by His Spirit, build that capsule around you and protect you from all that is happening in the outside world. If you will walk in the Word, you can be protected at all times and the wicked one will not be able to touch you. That capsule is the shield of faith. *"Faith cometh by hearing, and hearing by the word of God"* (Romans 10:17).

Faith works by love. The Bible says in Ephesians 6:16 that faith quenches *all* the fiery darts of the wicked one— not part of them, *all* of them. The first time I heard Brother

Kenneth Hagin say this, I was thrilled! He spoke to Satan and said, "Satan, my household is off limits to you." Then he put up a sign in the world of the spirit that said, "Off limits, Satan. This means you!" Glory to God! I had always thought that Satan held the key to my back door and could come and go as he pleased. Then I found out about my authority as a believer.

Developing Faith in God's Love

You might ask, "How do you know when your faith is developed in a certain area?" The same rules apply to the development of faith in every area of life. Faith is faith in any Bible subject—whether it is the new birth, the infilling of the Holy Ghost, right-standing with God, divine health, divine prosperity or some other area. It is the same spiritual substance. It works the same in every situation.

(1) *Put the Word of God first place. Don't be moved by feelings.* To develop your faith in God's love, or in anything else from God, you have to learn what the Word says about it. *"Faith cometh by hearing, and hearing by the word of God"* (Romans 10:17). For instance, Psalm 23:6 says, *"Surely goodness and mercy shall follow me all the days of my life."* Put that Word first place. Don't ever go by how you feel about the love of God. Don't confess anything else. Be confident in the fact that God's mercy and goodness follow you all the

days of your life. You should read 1 John over and over on a regular basis.

(2) *Meditate on the scriptures concerning God's love.* Meditation develops the capacity for faith. As you meditate in God's Word and your capacity begins to grow, you will recognize the power God's love can have in your life. Then the things of Satan will begin to shrink and lose their grip over your life as you realize the fullness of God's Word.

(3) *Act on the Word concerning the love of God.* First John 4:11-12 says, *"Beloved, if God so loved us, we ought also to love one another. No man hath seen God at any time. If we love one another, God dwelleth in us, and his love is perfected in us."* By practicing this love on one another, the love of God is perfected in us.

The Word *perfected* means "allowed to run its full course." You can let God's love run its full course in your life. Love never fails. Here we are again, reaching for that zero failure rate. It is possible, and it *will* come to pass! How are we going to do it? Not by becoming perfect ourselves, but by acting on the Word of God and allowing the love of God, which is perfect, to run its full course in our lives.

(4) *Decide to live the love life. Make the quality decision to live by love.* To develop your faith in divine healing, you have to make the decision to be well or you never will be healed. A quality decision is a necessity in learning to live the love life.

What is a quality decision? A decision from which there is no retreat. It simply means this: "With God in heaven as my helper, He that is within me is greater than he that is in the world. I refuse to allow anything to hinder me from walking in love. I make the quality decision now to walk the love walk, whether anyone else does or not."

It is a necessity that we renew our minds to the supernatural power of the love of God. We must develop our faith and renew our minds so we respond in love without having to think about it. We must learn to live in love, walk in love, talk in love and edify one another in love. Then, when the pressures come, when the hard times come, when disasters approach us, we won't have to stop and think. We will immediately react in love.

The secret to successful combat against Satan is to retaliate in the spirit, not in the natural. The love walk is 100 percent in the spiritual realm. This is where God wants the Body of Christ to walk. By developing our faith in the love of God, it will work and bring about the zero failure rate.

Now say this: *O God in heaven, I commit myself today to develop my faith in Your love. I commit myself to Your Word, to be pleasing unto You—to walk in love, even as Jesus walked. I make the quality decision now to talk in love, think in love and respond to all things in love. I renounce selfishness in the Name of Jesus. It has no part in me. I am born of love, so I will walk in love!*

Rooted and Grounded in Love

First John 2:5 says, *"But whoso keepeth his word, in him verily is the love of God perfected."*

There are two ways to perfect the love of God in your life:

1. By keeping the Word of God.
2. By practicing love on others.

Love takes practice, and we can practice on each other. You won't operate perfectly in love at the very beginning; but as you persist, you will get increasingly better at it. If you fail, simply confess it as sin, receive your forgiveness and go on. Keep loving. Keep overlooking the shortcomings of other people. Look for Jesus in them.

We must practice love until we are supporting one another. That way when one of us is down, the others will be up, and we will keep ourselves operating on a high plane at all times. The Bible says one can put a thousand to flight, two can put ten thousand to flight (Deuteronomy 32:30). We are many times greater and stronger when we join together in harmony and agreement. Together, we can do it!

Keep overlooking the shortcomings of other people. Look for Jesus in them.

In Ephesians 3:16-19, the Apostle Paul prays:

That he would grant you, according to the riches of his glory, to be strengthened with might by his Spirit in the inner man; that Christ may dwell in your hearts by faith; that ye, being rooted and grounded in love, may be able to comprehend with all saints what is the breadth, and length, and depth, and height; and to know the love of Christ, which passeth knowledge.

God has promised us the knowledge of His love. First John 4:16 says, *"And we have **known and believed** the love that God hath to us."* Believing that love is acting on it. Putting it into operation. When we do, we reach out into areas that pass human knowledge.

Again, Ephesians 3:17 says, *"That Christ may dwell in your hearts by faith; that ye, being rooted and grounded in love..."*

We are to be *rooted* and *grounded* in the love of God. In His parable of the sower, Jesus said,

And these are they by the way side, where the word is sown; but when they have heard, Satan cometh immediately, and taketh away the word that was sown in their hearts. And these are they likewise which are sown on stony ground; who, when they have heard the word, immediately receive it with gladness; And have no root in themselves, and so endure but for a time: afterward, when affliction or persecution ariseth for the word's sake, immediately they are offended (Mark 4:15-17).

They heard the Word with gladness, but when the persecution and affliction came for the Word's sake, they were offended. They didn't respond in the love of God. They responded in the natural realm, and Satan stole all the Word that was in them. They were not rooted in love.

God is declaring unto you and me that we can have a comprehensive revelation of Christ's love—its height, its depth, its width and its breadth. To know His love is to know God because He *is* love. God is telling us, "I'll teach you all there is to know about Me." He has been wanting, since the beginning of time, to share Himself with us—not part, but *all!* Think about that! God is offering you and me understanding of the height, depth, width and breadth of *Himself.* It's almost unbelievable, but it is true.

Developing the God Kind of Love

John 15:7-12 says:

If you abide in me, and my words abide in you, you shall ask what you will, and it shall be done unto you. Herein is my Father glorified, that ye bear much fruit; so shall ye be my disciples. As the Father hath loved me, so have I loved you; continue ye in my love. If ye keep my commandments, ye shall abide in my love; even as I have kept my Father's commandments, and abide in his love. These things have I spoken unto you, that my joy might remain in you, and that your joy might be full. This is my commandment, That ye love one another, as I have loved you.

We are to walk *even as* Jesus walked. We are to forgive *even as* He forgives. We are to abide in His love *even as* He abides in the Father's love.

How do you live, walk, forgive and love even as Jesus does? Only one way: by faith. It takes spiritual power and spiritual understanding to walk in love because the faith realm is beyond the natural realm, beyond what the mind can grasp.

The love of God was put in us at the time of the new birth. We can love with the Jesus kind of love and operate in the Jesus kind of faith. The Bible says it is the faith of God that has been imparted to our spirits. It is *God's* faith. If you didn't have the capacity for it, God wouldn't have given it to you in the first place. He certainly would not have commanded us to walk in something for which we didn't have the capacity.

The new birth is what gives us the capacity for God's love and God's faith. An unregenerate man cannot walk in this kind of power. We know this from Jesus' words in Mark 2:22, *"And no man putteth new wine into old bottles: else the new wine doth burst the bottles, and the wine is spilled, and the bottles will be marred: but new wine must be put into new bottles."* A spirit that is not born again cannot contain the power of God.

When men came in contact with the tangible power of Almighty God in the old covenant, they were killed. In 2 Samuel 6, a man was struck dead when he touched the Ark of the Covenant. The power of God was too strong for his physical body. You, as a born-again believer, could pick up the Ark of the Covenant and walk off with it. You have the capacity to operate in that power. Why? Because you are born of that power. That power re-created your spirit.

His commandment is for us to go into all the world and preach the gospel to every creature and, in His Name, cast out demons, lay hands on the sick and they will recover and make disciples of nations. This is the way He gave this commandment— that we should practice this love *on* one another, *with* one another, *for* one another. We are responsible for loving one another, *even as* Jesus has loved us.

We are responsible for loving one another, even as Jesus loved us.

This is not just for the original apostles. This is a commandment to the whole Body of Christ. Consequently, we can conclude that the whole Body of Christ has this God kind of love. We are commanded to walk in it, to keep His Word and to walk *even as* He walked.

Let's go to Ephesians 5:1-2 and find out how: *"Be ye therefore followers of God as dear children: And walk in love, as Christ also hath loved us, and hath given himself for us an offering and a sacrifice to God for a sweet smelling savour."*

The Greek word translated "follower" in this scripture is *mimetes*. We get our English words *imitate* and *mimic* from it. So let's read it that way. *"Be ye therefore, [imitators] of God, as dear children."* We are to imitate God the way children imitate their parents. What does it mean to imitate God? It means to act like Him, talk like Him and walk like Him. *To walk as He walked* means to imitate Him in every realm of life—daily conduct, daily thoughts, daily conversations. How can we ever do that? Jesus said, "If you've seen Me, you've seen the Father." (See John 14:9.)

What can we say about the way Jesus has loved us? Let's take His earthly ministry as an example. What did He do? Acts 10:38 says, *"...who went about doing good, and healing all that were oppressed of the devil."* To walk as He walked means getting involved with other people, with their problems and situations. We must come to the place where we are ready to give ourselves to one another. Jesus gave of Himself in His earthly ministry. When you made Jesus your Lord, you entered into that ministry. Now, you are called to give of yourself. As a Christian you are called to be a "little Christ." To walk in your calling, you have to walk in the love of God. If you listen to your body or your mind, you will never fulfill what God intends for your life.

There is an area in the giving of yourself that some people misunderstand. It is not right for a person to go on and on and on, working endlessly, until he works himself to exhaustion. You can reach a place physically that makes you ineffective spiritually. At that point you are no longer giving yourself to others, you are a burden to them.

When you are studying the love of God, you must *always* remember one thing: God is love. Love is God, Himself. Walking in love is walking in God. You should allow God to run His full course in your life. His full course is not for you to jump out of the boat, take one or two steps on the water, and then sink. His full course is for you to walk all the way out to Jesus and all the way back to the boat!

Someone might say, "Now wait a minute. If I walked in the love of God and started loving with this Jesus kind of love, I would be like a lamb to the slaughter. You don't know the kind of people I live and work with!"

Walking in God's love does not mean just becoming a lamb to the slaughter. Romans 8:36 says, *"As it is written, For thy sake we are killed all the day long; we are accounted as sheep for the slaughter."* It does not say we *are* sheep for the slaughter; it says we are *accounted as* sheep for the slaughter. By whom? God? No. By the rest of the world. When you act in the love of God, the whole world will look at you, scratch their heads and say, "There's got to be something wrong with you! If I acted that way, everybody in town would run all over me." The world will account you as sheep for the slaughter. They don't know God and the power of His love. The only love the world knows is human love; and human love is selfish, possessive and spiritually bankrupt.

The Power of God's Love

By walking in God's love, you release a force to work in your behalf—a force that has all the appearance of weakness but is stronger than any force in existence. To walk in love is to step aside and allow the power of the universe to come between you and the situation with which you are dealing.

> *To walk in love is to step aside and allow the power of the universe to come between you and the situation with which you are dealing.*

Romans 8:37 says, *"Nay…"* In other words, "No, you are not a lamb to the slaughter." It says, *"Nay, in all these things we are* **more than conquerors."** You are more than a conqueror! It is one thing to conquer; it is another thing entirely to conquer and *occupy!* Praise God!

You are one spirit with the Lord. Glory to God! He paid the price so you wouldn't have to pay it. You didn't have to go to the Cross. He went there for you. You are more than a conqueror through Him who loved you—through the power of that love. There is an unseen power that goes into operation when a person is developed in the love of God and knows how to walk in it. When the world starts to run over you because you appear to be weak, they will run into the unseen power. It's all around you. It's in you—ever ready for whatever comes. God wants you to be full of the Word and use His Name without fear. It is yours to use. And God will back you with His power just like He said He would.

One of the most outstanding examples of the power of God's love was manifest during Jesus' ministry. In John 8, Jesus was confronted by some Jews as He was teaching in the temple. His words were so forceful in the face of their traditional thinking that they were angered. Verse 59 says, *"Then took they up stones to cast at him: but Jesus hid himself, and went out of the temple, going through the midst of them, and so passed by."*

Jesus just turned around and walked through the midst of the crowd. They were trying to stone Him and He walked off! They couldn't even see Him! This verse says He hid Himself. He was protected by an invisible shield—the love of God.

I have seen men walk in that kind of protection, and I have walked in it myself from time to time. It is the protective shield of God's love behind which every believer can walk, but very few know how. Jesus said, *"Strait is the gate, and narrow is the way, which leadeth unto life, and few there be that find it"* (Matthew 7:14). But thank God for the few who do! I have made up my mind to be one of those!

To walk in love is to walk in the very highest spiritual realm there is. Jesus walked in that realm. We have seen it operate in His earthly ministry. Another example of the power of God's love is found in Acts 7. It is the story of Stephen as he stands before the high priest, accused of blasphemy. Acts 6 describes him as *"a man full of faith and of the Holy Ghost."* It says, *"Stephen, full of faith and power, did great wonders and miracles among the people."*

Stephen preached the gospel as his defense, and his accusers were outraged:

> When they heard these things, they were cut to the heart, and they gnashed on him with their teeth. But he, being full of the Holy Ghost, looked up stedfastly into heaven, and saw the glory of God, and Jesus standing on the right hand of God, And said, Behold, I see the heavens opened, and the Son of man standing on the right hand of God. Then they cried out with a loud voice, and stopped their ears, and ran upon him with one accord, and cast him out of the city, and stoned him: and the witnesses laid down their clothes at a young man's feet, whose name was Saul. And they stoned Stephen, calling upon God, and saying, Lord Jesus, receive my spirit. And he kneeled down, and cried with a loud voice, Lord, lay not this sin to their charge. And when he had said this, he fell asleep (Acts 7:54-60).

Stephen was demonstrating the love of God. He said

what Jesus said at Calvary, *"Father, forgive them, for they
know not what they do."* Stephen showed that he had the
same capacity to love as Jesus did. The love of God was
perfected in his life. He imitated Jesus.

How did Stephen learn? By waiting on tables. By serving
people. Through Stephen and his ministry, great miracles
were performed. Where were they done? Among the people.

First John 5:1, 4-5 says:

Whosoever believeth that Jesus is the Christ is born of
God: and every one that loveth him that begat loveth
him also that is begotten of him. For whatsoever is
born of God overcometh the world: and this is the
victory that overcometh the world, even our faith.
Who is he that overcometh the world, but he that
believeth that Jesus is the Son of God?

God is love and we are born of love. Every born-again
believer on the face of this earth is a world-overcomer. He
is not in the process of overcoming the world; he *is* a
world-overcomer. You can be a world-overcomer and never
overcome. You can be a rich man and starve to death. You
are a creature with a will and a choice. You may never realize it in your own life, but as far as God is concerned, you
have already overcome.

Let's read Romans 5:3-5:

And not only so, but we glory in tribulations also: knowing that tribulation worketh patience; and patience, experience; and experience, hope: and hope maketh not ashamed; because the love of God is shed abroad in our hearts by the Holy Ghost which is given unto us.

We know definitely that we have the same capacity to love as Jesus does because it is the love of God which has been shed abroad in our hearts by the Holy Spirit. Think about that. The love of God is shed abroad in *your* heart. It is in you because He is in you. You are *born* of Him. You have been made one spirit with the Lord. What is that spirit? The Holy Spirit. Who is He? He is compassion and mercy and love.

Words and Actions

You can respond in love in every situation and with every person you meet by the confession of your mouth and by your actions.

How can you become "love-of-God conscious" to the point that you respond in love in every situation and with every person you meet?

There are two ways: by the confession of your mouth and by your actions.

Let's talk a moment about acting on and confessing the love of God.

First John 4:15 says, *"Whosoever shall confess that Jesus is the Son of God, God dwelleth in him, and he in God."* As we confess the Word concerning the love of God and act in accordance with our confession, it becomes a reality in our lives and affects our consciousness.

In the Sermon on the Mount, Jesus said, *"Why take ye thought saying...."* Take the thought and say it! The more you confess the Word of God, the more you deposit that Word into your spirit. Once you get it down in you in abundance, it will begin to flow out. When it comes from your spirit, and then out of your mouth, it will come in the form of faith-filled words.

Jesus said, *"A good man out of the good treasure of the heart bringeth forth good things: and an evil man out of the evil treasure bringeth forth evil things"* (Matthew 12:35).

The things coming to pass in your life are the result of what is in your heart. Your heart is the clearinghouse. The only way things can come out of your heart is through your mouth. First, you speak it forth; then, your words and actions license a spiritual agency to bring into existence what you say.

There are two spiritual agencies functioning in the earth. One is headed by Satan, the other is headed by Jesus. Satan's realm includes the principalities, powers, rulers of darkness of this world and wicked spirits in heavenly places (Ephesians 6:12). Jesus' realm includes the angels of God which have been sent forth to minister for the heirs of salvation (Hebrews 1:14).

When you speak words, you license either Satan's agency or Jesus' agency to support these words. *You* are the establishing witness.

When you say, "Every time the flu comes to town I get it," you are not licensing the angels of God, you are licensing Satan and his agents. Then your actions support your words and give him continuous access to your affairs. When the flu season comes, you go to the drugstore and buy nine boxes of pills and all the cold medicine you can get. Your actions have supported your words.

On the other hand, the angels of God will back your words when you speak in line with the Word of God. When you fill your heart with God's words, you will speak them out of your mouth. Your confession will be, "By His stripes, I'm healed. I'm redeemed from the curse of sickness. Jesus bore my sicknesses and carried my diseases. I will *not* have the flu."

Confessing God's Word with your mouth is an exercise of faith. You may have to believe your way out of the flu several times before your faith is fully developed; but every time you say it, you knock Satan and his flu back about 14 yards. The key is to keep saying it, to keep walking in it. The day will arrive when you will be through with the flu forever. The Word of God is not subject to your failures. It is true regardless of circumstances or situations.

The speed with which the words work and the progress of your spiritual growth are in direct proportion to the amount of time you spend at it. Jesus said in John 15:7, *"If ye abide in me, and my words abide in you, **ye shall ask what ye will,** and it shall be done unto you."* There is no shortcut. You *must* take the time and fill your heart with God's Word. *Take the Word and say it.*

A key phrase in operating this principle is, "In the Name of Jesus." By using Jesus' Name, you license all the angels of heaven to protect you and watch over God's Word to perform it in your life. It is essential that you keep your actions *in line* with that. By keeping your actions and your confession *in line* with the Word, the desired result will come to pass.

Now let's look at 1 Corinthians 13:4-8:

[Now love] suffereth long, and is kind; [love] envieth not; [love] vaunteth not itself, is not puffed up, doth not behave itself unseemly, seeketh not her own, is not easily provoked, thinketh no evil; rejoiceth not in iniquity, but rejoiceth in the truth; beareth all things, believeth all things, hopeth all things, endureth all things. [Love] never faileth.

Remember, God is love. Let's read these verses putting God in love's place and we will receive insight into His nature.

[God] suffereth long, and is kind; [God] envieth not;
[God] vaunteth not [Himself], is not puffed up, [God]
doth not behave Himself unseemly, [He] seeketh not
[His] own, is not easily provoked, thinketh no evil;
[God] rejoiceth not in iniquity, but rejoiceth in the truth;
[He] beareth all things, believeth all things, hopeth all
things, endureth all things. [God] never faileth.

As believers, we are born of God. Because God is love,
we are born of love. The Bible says we are to imitate God. It
says we are to love even as He loved. So let's read this in the
first person and make it our confession of love:

"I suffer long and am kind. I envy not. I vaunt not myself.
I am not puffed up. I do not behave myself unseemly. I seek
not my own. I am not easily provoked. I think no evil. I rejoice
not in iniquity, but rejoice in the truth. I bear all things, believe
all things, hope all things, endure all things. I never fail."

Take these scriptures of love and write them down.
Begin to confess them on a daily basis. Confess them over
and over again, injecting your own name.

I've heard the love walk described this way. "To walk in
love—to live in this God kind of love—is like a man walking in a dense, early morning fog. He walks in it until his
clothes are saturated with moisture, until the brim of his
hat drips with water." You can walk in the love of God to
the point that your whole being is saturated with love.

Every word you speak drips with love, and everybody you come into contact with is affected by that love. Hallelujah!

I have set myself and am determined to be "Holy Spirit possessed." I intend for Him to operate totally, completely and absolutely in my life. It's my will that He do it. I'm not submitting to Him to do just the things I want or just the things I don't want. I'm submitting to Him to do whatever He desires—in any way He desires. I have made up my mind to come to that place in love—to be totally and completely filled with the Holy Spirit in every area of my being. In order to do that, I must have a revelation of the love of God, and I must walk in it.

You can walk in the love of God to the point that your whole being is saturated with love.

Make this confession now. Read it out loud. "I'm a believer. I'm born of love. The love way is my way because it's God's way and I am born of God."

Keeping Yourself in Love

Who shall separate us from the love of Christ? shall tribulation, or distress or persecution, or famine, or nakedness, or peril, or sword?...For I am persuaded, that neither death, nor life, nor angels, nor principalities, nor powers, nor things present, nor things to come, Nor height, nor depth, nor any other creature, shall be able to separate us from the love of God, which is in Christ Jesus our Lord (Romans 8:35, 38-39).

There is nothing that can separate you from the love of God. God will never fall out of love with you. His love is

God won't fall out of love with you, but you can separate yourself from His love.

never ending. It is eternal. No matter how deep into sin you get, God will always love you. Some parents say to their children, "Don't be a bad boy. Jesus won't love you if you're bad." What a lie! Don't use God or Jesus as your whipping boy!

Who shall separate us from the love of Christ? Shall tribulation? Shall distress? Shall persecution? Shall famine? Shall nakedness? Peril? Sword? No, on every count!

Who can separate you from the love of Christ? Only one person: you. God won't fall out of love with you, but you can separate yourself from His love.

Jude 19-21 says:

These be they who separate themselves, *sensual*, having not the Spirit. But ye, beloved, building up yourselves on your most holy faith, praying in the Holy Ghost, keep yourselves in the love of God, looking for the mercy of our Lord Jesus Christ unto eternal life.

If you separate yourself from God's love, you will get *sensual*. It doesn't mean you are mad at God or you are out into sin, but you are not in close fellowship with the Father. Now when you get into the sensual area, you can easily get off into sin. First, you begin to deceive yourself. According to James 1:22, a man who is a hearer of the Word and not a doer is self-deceived. You will begin to hear things that you thought were God when it was actually your carnal mind.

Men have based their ministry on things that were a result of their own carnal thinking. They stand up in the pulpit and say, "After I had my heart attack and was lying there on my back in the hospital, I said, 'God, why did this happen to me?' And God spoke to me and said, 'I put that heart attack on you to slow you down and teach you something.'" That was not God! No. They heard their own self-deceived carnal minds say it. They drew a conclusion based on their circumstances and called it a "word from the Lord." It is a very dangerous thing to attempt to answer spiritual questions out of natural human thinking.

Keeping yourself in God's love takes effort and discipline. It won't be easy, but it's worth it. You will need to continually remind yourself of the commitment you made at the time of your conversion. Entering into the new birth is entering into the power of God's love. You are now born of that love and are to manifest it in every area of your life.

In Ephesians 4, the Apostle Paul gave specific instructions on how you are to walk in that powerful love.

Verse 25: *"Wherefore putting away lying, speak every man truth with his neighbour: for we are members of one another."* This is how the Word says you are to treat your neighbor.

The golden rule says, "Do unto others as you would have them do unto you." This is not just a good rule. Jesus spoke it during the Sermon on the Mount. *"Therefore all things whatsoever ye would that men should do to you, do ye even so to them: for this is the law and the prophets"* (Matthew 7:12).

It is spiritual law that what you do to others is what they are going to do to you. There is an uncanny, spiritual balance that takes place. When a man lives hard and is hard on the people around him, he will be the most miserable guy in the world. Jesus said if you live by the sword, you will die by the sword (Matthew 26:52). It is spiritual law that you reap what you sow. There is only one way to break that: Stop it with the Word of God and the Name of Jesus through active repentance. To repent means to turn and go the other way.

The law of reaping and sowing will work *for* you or *against* you. To a giver, it is the greatest law God has ever put into operation. The person who walks in love has something to look forward to in this life.

Verse 26: *"Be ye angry, and sin not: let not the sun go down upon your wrath."* How do you sin when you are angry? Two ways: (1) with your mouth and (2) with your actions. Don't act on anger, just stand on the Word of God and keep your mouth shut. Don't stay mad past sundown. "But you don't know what they did to me!" I don't care what they did to you. Don't let it go past sundown! God is telling you how to walk in love where your neighbors are concerned.

Verse 27: *"Neither give place to the devil."* To whom is this written? The believer. We are to give Satan no place!

Verse 28: *"Let him that stole steal no more: but rather let him labour, working with his hands the thing which is good, that he may have to give to him that needeth."* This tells you why you are working at your job. The reason you labor with your hands is in order to be a giver. God intends to meet your need out of the return on your giving. *"He that hath pity upon the poor lendeth unto the Lord; and that which he hath given will he pay him again"* (Proverbs 19:17). You can't over-tax God with your need, no matter what it is. He wants to lavish things on you—a hundred times more than you could get by working. The Word says, *"...the eyes of the Lord run to and fro throughout the whole earth, to show himself strong in the behalf of them whose heart is perfect toward him"* (2 Chronicles 16:9).

God is a giver. The Word says in Ephesians 2:6-7:

[He] hath raised us up together, and made us sit together in heavenly places in Christ Jesus: that in the ages to come he might show the exceeding riches of his grace in his kindness toward us through Christ Jesus.

Verse 10 says, *"We are his workmanship, created in Christ Jesus unto good works, which God hath before ordained that we should walk in them."* He created the universe for one child—Jesus—and because we are in Him, we can share in His blessings.

Verse 29: *"Let no corrupt communication proceed out of your mouth, but that which is good to the use of edifying, that it may minister grace unto the hearers."* Here is a law you can use to discipline your mouth: Corrupt communication includes gossip, profanity, bad news and negativism. Don't let it come out of your mouth.

There is an excellent rule to use in governing your vocabulary with love: Does it minister grace? If it doesn't, don't say it. Grace is an act of God's love. Stop and ask yourself, "Will my words minister undeserved favor to the person to whom I am talking?" Even though it may be true, if it doesn't minister grace to the hearer, don't say it.

When you open your mouth and speak with the grace

> *When you open your mouth and speak with the grace of God, God will back your words.*

of God, God will back your words. When you speak words that are in line with God's Word, then all of heaven pays attention. The angels of God are commissioned to see that those things which you say come to pass. When you speak words of faith, the angels will move in your behalf; but they cannot back words of hate, strife, unbelief, selfishness, etc. When you speak words that are not of grace and love, you violate the commandment of God. That is when Satan will go to work. God can't cause your words to come to pass because He is not the author of sickness or fear or strife. But Satan is! By speaking those words, you license Satan to move in your life.

When you hear corrupt communication, you may have to turn and walk away rather than get involved. Guard your tongue, and don't talk about other people.

Verses 30-32: *"And grieve not the Holy Spirit of God, whereby ye are sealed unto the day of redemption. Let all bitterness, and wrath, and anger, and clamour, and evil speaking, be put away from you, with all malice: and be ye kind one to another, tenderhearted, forgiving one another, even as God for Christ's sake hath forgiven you."* This is how we are to deal with our neighbors and with one another in the Body of Christ.

Ephesians 4 is vital in our study of God's love. The entire chapter deals with keeping harmony in the Body of Christ. I suggest you spend time meditating on these scriptures; allow them to go deep into your spirit.

The Power of Forgiveness

Jesus places a tremendous importance on harmony and agreement between believers. Forgiveness plays a vital role in living that life of love and harmony in the earth today.

There is great power in forgiveness. We are to forgive, *even as* God for Christ's sake has forgiven us.

How does God forgive? Does He forgive but never forget? No, God's way of forgiving is to forgive *and* forget. When God forgets, He does not just set it aside. He completely wipes it away. It no longer exists in His consciousness.

To forgive others as God forgives us requires an act of faith. God's forgiveness is the supernatural ability to totally eradicate from your consciousness any thought or memory of an incident.

There is a realm of forgiveness in which every believer can walk. It cannot be done through your own natural ability. It is a supernatural act in which you exercise your faith, the love of God and the power of forgiveness until that incident is completely and totally eradicated from your consciousness just as it is from God's. Every believer must learn how to live and walk in that realm of forgiveness.

Jesus makes the act of forgiveness an integral part of the faith life. Let's look at Mark 11:22-24. This has to be the most well-known scripture reference there is on the subject of faith. Jesus is teaching about the God kind of faith and how it operates:

> Have faith in God. For verily I say unto you, That whosoever shall say unto this mountain, Be thou removed, and be thou cast into the sea; and shall not doubt in his heart, but shall believe that those things which he saith shall come to pass; he shall

have whatsoever he saith. Therefore I say unto you, What things soever ye desire when ye pray, believe that ye receive them, and ye shall have them.

Now notice His words in verses 25-26:

And when ye stand praying, forgive, if ye have aught against any: that your Father also which is in heaven may forgive you your trespasses. But if you do not forgive, neither will your Father which is in heaven forgive your trespasses.

In verse 26, He very plainly states a spiritual law: If you do not forgive, then your Father in heaven will not forgive you.

In Matthew 18:21, Peter asked Jesus how many times he should forgive his brother. Jesus answered, *"Until seventy times seven."* (That's 490 times!) Then He relates a parable:

Therefore is the kingdom of heaven likened unto a certain king, which would take account of his servants. And when he had begun to reckon, one was brought unto him, which owed him ten thousand talents. But forasmuch as he had not to pay, his lord commanded him to be sold, and his wife, and children, and all that he had, and payment to be made. The servant therefore fell down, and worshipped him,

saying, Lord, have patience with me, and I will pay
thee all. Then the lord of that servant was moved
with compassion, and loosed him, and forgave him
the debt. But the same servant went out, and found
one of his fellowservants, which owed him an hundred pence: and he laid hands on him, and took him
by the throat, saying, Pay me that thou owest. And
his fellowservant fell down at his feet, and besought
him, saying, Have patience with me, and I will pay
thee all. And he would not: but went and cast him
into prison, till he should pay the debt. So when his
fellowservants saw what was done, they were very
sorry, and came and told unto their lord all that was
done. Then his lord, after that he had called him,
said unto him, O thou wicked servant, I forgave thee
all that debt, because thou desirest me: shouldest
not thou also have had compassion on thy
fellowservant, even as I had pity on thee? And his
lord was wroth, and delivered him to the tormentors, till he should pay all that was due unto him. So
likewise shall my heavenly Father do also unto you,
if ye from your hearts forgive not every one his
brother their trespasses (Matthew 18:23-35).

God looks at unforgiveness as wickedness. This parable
shows the consequences of walking in unforgiveness. The
servant was forgiven of a large debt, but then would not

release his fellowservant of a small, insignificant debt. His attitude of unforgiveness cost him much more than the debt he owed. Verse 34 says his lord delivered him over to the tormentors until the debt was paid. Unforgiveness will place you directly in Satan's hands (2 Timothy 2:23-26).

There can be no room in your life for unforgiveness. If you are unwilling to forgive, you put yourself automatically in a position where Satan can torment and attack you. If someone does or says something to you that hurts, you usually try to shrug it off, but that is the kind of thing of which Satan will try to take advantage.

The little debts we don't forgive are what give Satan place in our lives—the small things we do and say, the cutting words and unkind remarks. Many times these incidents of aggravation occur with people in the world whom we don't know personally; they are easily forgotten, but never forgiven. These things may look unimportant but remember: We are commissioned to take the message of forgiveness to the world, not take it from them (2 Corinthians 5:18-19). God has forgiven us of a life of sin, yet we hold little things against each other.

As I was praying about this, the Spirit of God showed me what happens when we allow unforgiveness to build up in our spirits. I saw a pipe stretching between God and myself. The pipe was a funnel for the power of God. At God's end, there was a surge of power going in. At my end, there was only a trickle flowing out. The pipe was clogged with dirt and filth. The Lord explained that the filth was unforgiveness and had been put in the pipe (my spirit) one grain at a time. God was not holding back His power. It was flowing. The pipe was so clogged that His power could not flow through it.

It is so important to have a forgiving heart. In order for us as believers to effectively reach the world with the gospel—the good news of Jesus Christ—the power of God must be allowed to flow through us unhindered. We cannot be used by the Holy Spirit when our spirits are clogged with bitterness and resentment and unforgiveness. This places a serious responsibility on our shoulders. We must open ourselves to God and purge our hearts of all unforgiveness.

> But in a great house there are not only vessels of gold and of silver, but also of wood and of earth; and some to honour, and some to dishonour. If a man therefore purge himself from these, he shall be a vessel unto honour, sanctified, and meet for the master's use, and prepared unto every good work (2 Timothy 2:20-21).

Jesus knew the importance of forgiveness and that is why He connected it so closely with the operation of faith in Mark 11. Faith will not work in an unforgiving heart. Galatians 5:6 says faith works by love. If you are holding anything against another person, then it will hinder your faith. By harboring unforgiveness—no matter how small it may seem—you literally tie God's hands. Remember, Jesus said, "If you do not forgive, then the Father cannot forgive you." This is spiritual law.

Faith will not work in an unforgiving heart.

Every believer must have a forgiving heart. Only then will true harmony come into our homes and bring us into a position of total harmony with God and with one another. It is time for the Body of Christ to come to maturity in this area. For years we have concentrated on developing the faith walk. We have studied much about how to operate proficiently in faith. Now we must operate just as proficiently in forgiveness and love.

What I am sharing with you is spiritual truth. It is totally contrary to the world's way of thinking and goes against the grain of human behavior. To live and walk in forgiveness, you will have to resist pride. At times you will have to go to your brother and ask his forgiveness. You will have to forgive him, even though every ounce of your being wants to strike out against him. You will have to forgive others, even as God, for Christ's sake, has forgiven you.

Forgiveness requires an act of your will. You cannot depend on your feelings. Most of the time, you will have to forgive—not because you feel like it—but simply because the Word says you must.

It is a simple matter to purge or cleanse your spirit of

unforgiveness; you merely have to stand on the Word of faith.

1. Confess the sin of unforgiveness according to
   1 John 1:9.
2. Forgive as an act of your will and obedience, not
   your feelings. Forgive by faith and God will honor it.
3. Believe you receive forgiveness and cleansing from
   all unrighteousness—including any remembrance of
   being wronged. God's power is cleansing power. You
   are forgiven even as He forgave. It will cleanse your
   consciousness completely.
4. Praise God and give thanks that it is done. The act of
   praise is very important. You are a priest of God: you
   have been purged and cleansed. Now you are in the
   perfect position to offer a sacrifice of praise unto
   God (Hebrews 13:15).

If Satan brings a symptom of unforgiveness to you, resist
him by saying, "No, I have already forgiven that person by
faith, and I have received my forgiveness according to God's
Word. I refuse to remember it."

Make it your goal to develop and maintain an attitude of
forgiveness. See that you keep your heart clean before God.
Be quick to repent when you are faced with opportunities
for strife. Don't allow Satan any place in your life.

Use this confession of God's Word to activate the power

of love and close all doors to Satan. Keep the pipe clean and the power of God flowing!

"Father, in the Name of Jesus, I make a fresh commitment to You to live in peace and harmony—not only with my brothers and sisters in the Body of Christ, but with my friends and associates, neighbors and family.

"I let go of all bitterness, resentment, envying, strife and unkindness in any form. I give no place to the devil, in Jesus' Name.

"Now, Father, I ask Your forgiveness. By faith, I receive it. I am cleansed from all unrighteousness through Jesus Christ. As I forgive and release all who have wronged and hurt me, I ask You to forgive and release them. Deal with them in Your mercy and lovingkindness.

"From this moment on, I set myself to walk in love, to seek peace, to live in agreement and to conduct myself toward others in a manner that is pleasing to You.

"It is written in Your Word that the love of God has been shed abroad in my heart by the Holy Ghost. I believe Your love flows out from me to everyone with whom I come in contact. In Jesus' Name, I receive it done. Amen."

Strife—The Enemy of Love

God will never fall out of love with you, but you can separate yourself from the benefit of His love by walking out into strife. Strife is deadly! It is born of the mind of Satan.

I want you to see Satan's strategy against the Body of Christ. A group of believers—working together in faith and love, operating in the gifts of the Spirit, moving in the power of God—has the potential to destroy Satan's efforts. In order to stop them, he has to stop the move of the Holy Spirit in their midst. How can he do that? He could send nine different evil spirits to come against each gift of the Spirit, but that would be unnecessary. There is really only one thing he has to do: stir up strife. If he can cause strife among believers, he can stop the power of God.

If Satan can cause strife among believers, he can stop the power of God.

Getting into strife is the most dangerous thing you can do! Take authority over it at its very beginning. Don't wait until it has grown strong and then try to suppress it.

In 1 Corinthians 13:1-3, you can see the complete destruction strife can bring.

"Though I speak with tongues of men and angels, and have not charity, I am become as sounding brass, or a tinkling cymbal." When love is not operating in a congregation, the gift of tongues has no value. There may be a manifestation of tongues, but it will have no power. It will be as sounding brass—just a loud noise!

"And though I have the gift of prophecy, and understand all mysteries, and all knowledge; and though I have all faith, so that

I could remove mountains, and have not charity, I am nothing."
Without love, these gifts—prophecy, wisdom, knowledge,
faith—are for nothing.

*"And though I bestow all my goods to feed the poor, and
though I give my body to be burned, and have not charity, it
profiteth me nothing."* To give without love is a waste. There
will be no return. The supply line has been cut.

First Corinthians 3:1-3 shows us something very important about walking in love. Paul wrote:

I, brethren, could not speak unto you as unto spiritual,
but as unto carnal, even as unto babes in Christ. I have
fed you with milk, and not with meat: for hitherto ye
were not able to bear it, neither yet now are ye able.
For ye are yet carnal: for whereas there is among you
envying, and strife, and divisions, are ye not carnal,
and walk as men?

In a congregation where the love of God is absent,
revelation knowledge is stopped. Even though Paul had the
knowledge, he could not get it over to them. Where there is
strife, there is confusion and every evil work (James 3:16).

Become Love-Conscious

In studying the love of God, you must remember this:

Walking in love is not just "being nice." Jesus was love manifest in the flesh, but there were times when He didn't appear to be "nice." One time He called the people snakes. He said, *"Ye generation of vipers!"* (Matthew 23:33). Another time He called a Syrophenician woman a dog (Mark 7:27). It didn't sound very sweet, but His words were effective. They got her attention and penetrated her unbelief. When He got through to her, she quit begging, looked Him straight in the face and said, "Even the dogs get the crumbs." She let Him realize she wasn't leaving there without the deliverance of her daughter. Jesus then said, *"For this saying go thy way; the devil is gone out of thy daughter"* (verse 29).

Love is a way of life—a life of being love-conscious instead of self-conscious. If you are not being love-conscious, you will always take the selfish route. Being love-conscious does not come automatically, it requires training. The Word says we are to practice love. *"If we love one another, God dwelleth in us, and his love is perfected in us"* (John 4:12). As we love one another, God's love is perfected in us. Now you can see why walking in love is walking in the highest spiritual realm of existence— you are walking in God and God is walking in you.

Read Matthew, Mark, Luke and John and you will see the results of what walking in love can bring. A man stood in the bow of a boat and spoke to a storm at sea. He said, *"Peace, be still."* The wind calmed and the waves were stilled. That man walked with God. He was in God and God was in Him. His name is Jesus!

Jesus is the supreme example of love to the world. We can follow His example because we have the Holy Spirit within us. We are not perfect, but love is. It is up to us to set our faith and make the decision to obey the one commandment of love:

> And whatsoever we ask, we receive of him, because we keep his commandments, and do those things that are pleasing in his sight. And this is his commandment, That we should believe on the name of his Son Jesus Christ and love one another, as he gave us commandment (1 John 3:22-23).

Notice how this is worded. If you ask most Christians the one commandment Jesus gave, they will answer, "We are to love one another." That is true, but it is only half of the commandment. The first half is just as important as the second half. *"This is his commandment, That we should [1] believe on the name of his Son Jesus Christ, and [2] love one another, as he gave us commandment."*

This is the only commandment under the New Covenant. This one fulfills all of the others. If you love me, you won't steal from me. If you love me, you won't hurt me. You will love God with all your heart and your soul. When you walk in God's love, you will fulfill the law.

Whenever you exercise faith in the Name of Jesus, there is an opportunity to use the love of God. Faith and love run hand in hand.

If you are going to lay hands on the sick, you must do it in love because faith works by love. Ministry is the act of loving someone with God's love, not with human love.

If you attempt to love with human love, the results will not be the same. Human love has very little spiritual value. It breeds selfishness and possession. The love of God will allow you to be free. It will never oppress you. Possessiveness and the love of God never run together. The Name of Jesus will not function in a possessive, dominating atmosphere.

Jesus said, "*...If two of you shall agree on earth as touching any thing that they shall ask, it shall be done for them of my Father which is in heaven. For where two or three are gathered together in my name, there am I in the midst of them*" (Matthew 18:19-20). The Name of Jesus works when believers are operating in agreement and harmony together. When we begin to harmonize and walk in agreement as a Body—not just as one or two, here and there, but in agreement—nothing shall be impossible to us!

Walking the Love Walk

The entire New Covenant—all that it involves—is wrapped up in love. According to God's Word, we can walk in perfected love while we are here on this earth. God is love, so love itself is already perfect; but we have to allow God to express His perfection in our lives. We do that by keeping His Word.

There Is No Fear in Love

"There is no fear in love; but perfect love casteth out fear: because fear hath torment. He that feareth is not made perfect in love" (1 John 4:18). Walking in love will get rid of

fear. When you realize that you are walking in the commandment of God, there is nothing to be afraid of. Fear has no
authority over you.

A man born into this earth is filled with and ruled by
fear, but a man with a re-created spirit is born of and filled
with the love of God. When you were born again, you were
born of love and there is no fear in love. When love entered,
it cast that fear out of you. However, your heart will continue
to receive, store, and produce fear if fear is fed into it. You
have the substance of faith in your spirit, but if you don't
feed it with the Word of God, it will never develop. If you
keep practicing fear, talking fear, living fear, the Word of God
will be completely choked out of your spirit.

Fear is a spiritual force. When you talk fear, you get the
spiritual power working to your *disadvantage* instead of to
your *advantage.* Get rid of the fear. If you have a sensation of
fear around you, openly and boldly rebuke it on the spot.
Don't put up with it. Don't fool with it. *Fear hath torment.*
Who, in the Bible, is called the "tormentor"? Satan. The Bible
says that we have not been given a spirit of fear (2 Timothy
1:7). When you are dealing with fear, you're dealing with a
spirit. I absolutely refuse to make myself available to any
kind of spirit but the Holy Spirit of God and those that are in
allegiance to Him. I will not make my body, my mind, my
spirit or my words available to any evil force.

Whenever fear shows up, we should be so trained in the

Word of God that we rebuke it, repel it and stand against it in every Bible form available. Fear is one of Satan's choice weapons. Stop fear. Rebuke it. Renounce it. Every time it crosses your mind, say out loud: I am redeemed from fear. Jesus delivered me from fear (Galatians 3:13, 14; Hebrews 2:15).

The Bible says, *"Finally, brethren, whatsoever things are true, whatsoever things are honest, whatsoever things are just, whatsoever things are pure, whatsoever things are lovely, whatsoever things are of good report…think on these things"* (Philippians 4:8). Take those good thoughts and *say* them.

Fear is fed, through your intellect, down into your spirit. Remember, fear is not natural to the believer. It comes from the outside, in. In Matthew 6:28, 31, Jesus said, *"Why take ye thought for raiment?…Take no thought, saying, What shall we eat? or, What shall we drink? or, Wherewithal shall we be clothed?"*

How do you *take* a thought? Just because a thought comes into your mind, you are not required to *take it,* or accept it. The Bible says, *"Casting down imaginations, and every high thing that exalteth itself against the knowledge of God, and bringing into captivity every thought to the obedience of Christ"* (2 Corinthians 10:5). Jesus said, *"Take no thought, saying."* How do you take a thought? By *saying* it. In Matthew 12:34, Jesus said, *"…out of the abundance of the heart the mouth speaketh."* How do you get it down into your spirit? By *saying* it. You feed it from your mind into your spirit by taking the thought and saying it. Develop habits of *saying* the Word of God. Stop practicing fear by using it in your daily conversation. It is not from God, so you don't need it.

Angelic Protection

In this realm of walking in God's love, there is a place of protection where God, Himself, is on the scene. Not only is He present, He is also very active. When Israel walked in the covenant of God and kept the commandments, they had nothing to fear. The Word of God says:

> And it shall come to pass, if thou shalt hearken diligently unto the voice of the Lord thy God, to observe and to do all his commandments which I command thee.... The Lord shall cause thine enemies that rise up against thee to be smitten before thy face: they shall come out against thee one way, and flee before thee seven ways (Deuteronomy 28:1, 7).

Look at Hebrews 1:13, 14: *"But to which of the angels said he at any time, Sit on my right hand, until I make thine enemies thy footstool? Are they not all ministering spirits, sent forth to minister for them who shall be heirs of salvation?"*

There is an unseen force of the presence of God encompassing you. You are surrounded by an unseen army of

angels—God's ministering spirits—moving with you at all
times. When you are walking in love, this angelic force can
work best in your behalf—to protect
you and see that the full armor of God

When you are
walking in love,
the angelic force
can work best in
your behalf.

works and that your prayer life is
unhindered. When you walk in agreement with others, Jesus will be in the
midst of that agreement to see that it
comes to pass. It is the force of Almighty
God that will move people and change things.

"The weapons of our warfare are not carnal, but mighty
through God to the pulling down of strong holds" (2 Corinthians
10:4). The angelic powers are a part of our weaponry. They
are ministering spirits sent forth into the earth to minister
for the heirs of salvation. The word *salvation* in the New
Testament has more than one meaning. We use it most of
the time in the context of being born again. The word *save*
means "to be put in a sound condition." That is what hap-
pened when you were born again. It also means "healing"
and "deliverance from temporal evils." We are heirs of
God's deliverance, the deliverance wrought when He
raised Jesus from the dead. We are delivered from the
authority of darkness, from the regions of the damned,
and from the hand of Satan. Praise God!

In 2 Kings 6 the armies of the enemy surrounded the
city where Elisha was. His servant said, *"Alas, my master!*

how shall we do?" Elisha's answer was, *"Fear not: for they that be with us are more than they that be with them."* Then he prayed: *"Lord, I pray thee, open his eyes, that he may see. And the Lord opened the eyes of the young man; and he saw: and, behold, the mountain was full of horses and chariots of fire round about Elisha."* Elisha wasn't afraid. He knew the armies of God were there because his covenant with God promised they would be. He was walking by faith. Hebrews 1:7 says, *"And of the angels he saith, Who maketh his angels spirits, and his ministers a flame of fire."*

Those angels did not suddenly come into existence when the servant saw them with his eyes. They were there all the time. Elisha had already said, "There are more of us than there are of them."

When you walk in the love of God, you are walking in the commandment of God. Psalm 103:20 says, *"Bless the Lord, ye his angels, that excel in strength, that do his commandments, hearkening unto the voice of his word."* What is the one commandment of the New Testament, of the New Covenant? The commandment of love. When you speak and act on God's Word in love, you allow the angelic spirits to work in your behalf. If you don't, they won't!

Stay in love and agreement. First John 2:10 gives one of the benefits. *"He that loveth his brother abideth in the light, and there is none occasion of stumbling in him."* When you are walking in love, you are not going to stumble. You have God in you and around you. All the angels are garrisoned round about you to keep you from moving to the right or to the left.

When you respond in love, you make yourself vulnerable. That is why the angels are there. *"For he shall give his angels charge over thee, to keep thee in all thy ways. They shall bear thee up in their hands, lest thou dash thy foot against a stone"* (Psalm 91:11-12). When you walk in the power of love, you walk in a place of protection. God will see to you.

> He that dwelleth in the secret place of the most High shall abide under the shadow of the Almighty. I will say of the Lord, He is my refuge and my fortress: my God; in him will I trust. Surely he shall deliver thee from the snare of the fowler, and from the noisome pestilence. He shall cover thee with his feathers, and under his wings shalt thou trust: his truth shall be thy shield and buckler (Psalm 91:1-4).

Walking in the Realm of the Miraculous

Human beings are supernatural beings. Every person has a deep desire to walk in the supernatural. It is that desire which motivated you to reach out to God.

The First Step

The first time you ever touched the realm of the miraculous was when you were born again. Someone preached the Word of God to you. You called on the Name of Jesus and reached out into that realm. The experience of the new birth is the most miraculous event that will ever occur in your life. You were reborn from a death of trespass and sin and made alive unto God. You were re-created and made to be righteousness—a spotless child of the God of heaven and earth. *"Therefore if any man be in Christ, he is a new creature: old things are passed away; behold, all things are become new"* (2 Corinthians 5:17). You instantly became a new creature. One translation says you became "a new species of being that never existed before."

Some people have experienced only the new birth, not realizing God has provided much more. Many have taken a step further and experienced the infilling of the Holy Spirit with evidence of speaking with other tongues. *"And when the day of Pentecost was fully come, they were all with one accord in one place.... And they were all filled with the Holy Ghost, and began to speak with other tongues, as the Spirit gave them utterance"* (Acts 2:1, 4). With the Holy Spirit active in you, you have the ability to witness to the world of God's great power and love.

> *Some people have experienced only the new birth, not realizing God has provided much more.*

The Commitment

A few have decided to live in that realm, renewing their minds with the Word and separating themselves from the carnal ways of the world.

I beseech you therefore, brethren, by the mercies of God, that ye present your bodies a living sacrifice, holy, acceptable unto God, which is your reasonable service. And be not conformed to this world: but be ye transformed by the renewing of your mind, that ye may prove what is that good, and acceptable, and perfect, will of God (Romans 12:1-2).

This is the committed believer—one who has made the decision to be a holy vessel unto honor, sanctified and meet for the Master's use, prepared unto every good work (2 Timothy 2:21). A born-again child of God is bone of His bone and flesh of His flesh, joined one spirit with the Lord (Ephesians 5:30; 1 Corinthians 6:17).

Standing in Full Measure

This is the ultimate realm of God's power—the place where all phases of ministry come together and operate at their fullest capacity.

God has been dealing with me about walking in the fullness of the gifts of the Spirit. In my estimation, the best I have seen of spiritual gifts in operation has fallen short of what God wants to do.

I have been very blessed to see great and miraculous happenings, both in church congregations and out in the streets. I have seen the power of God in operation, but I have never yet walked away satisfied that God did everything He wanted to do. The time is coming and now is at hand for the fullness of the gifts of the Spirit to operate— for God to do what He has been wanting to do all these years. Jesus said, "...*The works that I do shall he do also; and greater works than these shall he do; because I go unto my Father*" (John 14:12). The things I am going to share with you now are the things that will put us in a position to walk in that fullness of greater works.

We haven't reached that place yet, but we are headed that way now. Glory to God! We have finally come to the place where many of us are joining together and worshiping God in unity. "*Till we all come in the unity of the faith, and of the knowledge of the Son of God, unto a perfect man, unto the measure of the stature of the fulness of Christ*" (Ephesians 4:13). That is one of the most important steps that has to happen.

> Now that he ascended, what is it but that he also descended first into the lower parts of the earth? He that descended is the same also that ascended up far above all heavens, that he might fill all things. And he gave some, apostles; and some, prophets; and some, evangelists; and some, pastors and teachers; for the perfecting of the saints, for the work of the ministry, for the edifying of the body of Christ (Ephesians 4:9-12).

God said this to me: *The time is coming, and even now is, for people to walk in the fullness of their callings.* No, the day of the apostle is not over. The day of the prophet is not over. The evangelist and the pastor are not the only two ministries left in operation. The day is coming soon when we will see people walk in apostolic and prophetic power. We will see people walk in the office of evangelist in such a way that it will shake and startle the world.

First Corinthians 12:28 refers to other ministries that have been set in the Body of Christ. *"And God hath set some in the church, first apostles, secondarily prophets, thirdly teachers, after that miracles, then gifts of healings, helps, governments, diversities of tongues."*

Some people are called primarily to one office of ministry, such as miracles or gifts of healings. There are offices where people are called just to do miracles. There are people set in the church to do nothing but minister healing to the congregation. Kathryn Kuhlman walked in that ministry. She preached to people who didn't know much about the Word. God called her to minister in the gifts of healing; and thank God, she accepted it!

There is an office of governments and an office of helps. The office of helps is the most underdeveloped ministry in the Body of Christ today. It is a vital ministry, just as real and necessary as the office of pastor. God is raising up men and women in these last days to walk in the fullness of helps and governments. He said to me, *I will bless them for their commitment to see My covenant established in the earth. They will be there watching as the dead are raised and the blind see and the lame walk!* Praise God!

The New Breed

Our job is to walk in love toward one another and walk in this magnificent realm of the miraculous.

Speaking the truth in love, [we] may grow up in him into all things, which is the head, even Christ: From whom the whole body fitly joined together and compacted by that which every joint supplieth, according to the effectual working in the measure of every part, maketh increase of the body unto the edifying of itself in love (Ephesians 4:15, 16).

In the Greek text, the word *edify* means "to charge," as you would "charge" a battery. As we edify one another in love, we pump ourselves full of power! By speaking the truth in love to each other, we grow up into Him in all things and walk the earth in full stature as believers.

Jesus is not coming back for a weak, sickly Church that has been defeated and beaten down by Satan. No, praise God, we are going out of here in a blaze of glory!

You can walk in the realm of the miraculous using the authority of God, but you will never do it until you put God's Word first place in your life and walk in love. That is the realm of the miraculous!

No one will ever be able to make this kind of step without first receiving the commandment of love as

You will never walk in the realm of the miraculous until you put God's Word first place in your life and walk in love.

exactly what it is—*the commandment of God!* It is just as wrong to break this commandment as it is to break the commandment that says, *"Thou shalt not covet," "Thou shalt not kill," "Thou shalt not commit adultery,"* or any of the other commandments of God. Keeping this commandment of love will keep you from breaking the others. Therefore, this one is more important than all the others combined.

As long as, in your thinking, the commandment of love is just a "take it or leave it" proposition, you will never walk in the power of God's love. The pressure is too great. The moment you attempt to step into the love life, Satan will put so much against you, you will never stay with it. That's why God gave us the instruction to love in the form of a command. We have no choice!

When we accept love as a command, it will become a bit in our mouths during those times of pressure. That takes love out of the realm of just something we do when we are loved, or when our feelings aren't hurt, and into the powerful realm of God's love. Once you have entered the realm of God's love, you love because you are committed to God's Word and His command of love is a reality in your heart.

Receiving love as a command demands that we love whether anyone else does or not. It is only fair, however, to remind you that God has never changed. He has already said, "...*If thou shalt hearken diligently unto the voice of the Lord thy God, to observe and to do all his commandments* [now, there is only one to observe and do] *which I command thee this day....and all these blessings shall come on thee, and overtake thee...*" (Deuteronomy 28:1-2). Then you will be walking by faith on the highest level there is. God's miraculous power will operate in you, and you will see great and mighty things take place.

You will be counted among "the new breed" that shall go forth to the world. You shall no longer walk as other Gentiles walk in the vanity of their minds, but you shall walk in love even as Jesus walked—men and women knowing their full rights and privileges in Christ Jesus. You shall rise up, proclaiming the mighty Name of Jesus and prepare the way of the Lord's coming!

God Is Love

God is love. It does not say that
God *has* love, it says He *is* love.

That is the key to all Bible revelation.
When Paul said, *"And to know the love of
Christ..."* he meant you will know God. The
love of Christ is the love of God. The love is
God. There is nothing in Jesus but God. If
there were, He's not Jesus—He would not
be the spotless, resurrected Son of the living
God. As a born-again believer, you have the
ability of God to know and understand His
great love, to know and understand Him.

It takes an understanding of God to walk
with Him and walk in His love, and to do the
job that He has for us to do. Paul prayed that

we *"may be able to comprehend with all saints what is the breadth, and length, and depth, and height; and to know the love of Christ..."* (Ephesians 3:18). We can intimately know the love of Christ.

What does *comprehend* mean? To understand. The knowledge of God passes *all* human understanding. Why? *"That ye might be filled with all the fulness of God. Now unto him that is able to do exceeding abundantly above all that we ask or think, according to the power that worketh in us"* (Ephesians 3:19-20). What power? The power that strengthens the inner man, the power that is rooted and grounded in love. Without being rooted and grounded in love, you will never fully accomplish what God has for you to do.

Love must be our first and greatest quest. Love must be

> *Love must be our first and greatest quest.*

the center of our time. It must be the center of our thinking. It must be our greatest quest because God has given us a commandment to love. It is the law of heaven and earth. James calls it the "royal law" (James 2:8). It is a commandment.

Love Is a Commandment

The commandment of the Church is to love one another. I asked the Lord one time, "What is Your definition of a commandment?" He said, *A commandment is an order from*

Me, from which there is no retreat, about which there is no choice. That is His commandment to us as believers.

In 1 John 3:23, He already said, *"That we should believe on the name of his Son Jesus Christ, and love one another, as he gave us commandment."* He did not say *maybe* it was this way. This is the way it is. Someone may say, "I thought we had 10 commandments to obey?" We have 11. You have not been exonerated from the other 10, but if you will make the commitment to love, you will automatically fulfill all the rest (Romans 13:10).

Love has dictated our total victory in Christ Jesus. He said, "I command you to love even as I love you." If we love one another, we walk in the light (1 John 2:10), and His love is perfected in us (1 John 4:12). Then that same life, that same light, that is in God will begin to flow through us, and as we minister it to one another in fellowship, it will grow to "exploding" proportions.

Jesus made a statement in John 13:34. He said, *"A new commandment I give unto you, That ye love one another...."* You may ask, "What is so new about that?" In Leviticus 19:18 it says, *"...love thy neighbour as thyself."* The new part that Jesus added is this: *"...love one another; as I have loved you"* (John 13:34). It doesn't end there. He prayed that the love God loved Him with would be in us (John 17:26). That means we not only have a commandment to fulfill, but we have been given the capacity to love with the same love God has.

In Romans 5:5, we see that the love of God is shed abroad in our hearts by the Holy Ghost. God's love is in you. When you receive Jesus as the Lord of your life, God takes up residence within you; and if God is in you, His love is in you, for He is love. The new birth has provided you with the capability to love like God loves. It is your will that will determine how developed you get in that love.

Your will determines everything you do. It determines your success or your failure. It opens or closes the door to your financial success. It determines everything you are, everything you have been, and everything you will ever be. No one can determine your life and its outcome but you. It takes a commandment to affect a person's will strongly enough to overcome their emotions.

The Lord reminded me of an illustration of this concerning the will. When I was a boy, my father traveled a lot. Whenever I could spend time with him, it was precious to me. It was quality time. He would say, "I'm going to wake you up early in the morning and we are going to go fishing." I would get so excited about it all that I would spend whatever amount of time it took to straighten up my fishing tackle and get it ready to go. I didn't want to forget a thing, so I would lay my clothes out and have everything in its place. There were times when I would get up before Dad and get dressed and lay down on top of the covers so that I wouldn't waste a minute when he called for me. When he did, I would jump out of bed, even though it was 4:00 a.m., grab the tackle box in one hand and my rod and reel in the other hand and off we would go.

On the other hand, if my father had come to me the night before and said, "I'm going to get you up early in the morning and we are going to work in the yard," it would have been a different story. He would have to call for me at least three times to wake me up. I would think of every-thing I could to excuse myself from working in the yard. Now, if he would have walked out in the yard and said, "Put the lawnmower away and let's go fishing," it wouldn't have taken me any time at all to put the lawnmower away, get my rod and reel, and go. My will made the difference. It actually controlled my mind and my body.

When I played football as a young man, I worked in a bottling plant. One of the team member's father worked there and got several of us jobs during the summer so that we could stay in shape. We unloaded boxcars and stacked boxes full of bottles. In the afternoons, about 3:30 or 4:00, I would begin thinking, *I'll be so glad when I get through here today. I'm going home to bed.* Some of the other boys would plan to go out in the evening. They would ask me to go with them and I would tell them that I didn't want to go, that I was going home and going straight to bed. I would think, *I just can't wait until I get home. I am going to take a shower and get plenty of sleep tonight.*

Just before quitting time, at 5 p.m., I felt better. By the time I would get home and shower, I would say. "I'll get some sleep tomorrow night. I'm going out tonight." This is an excellent example of a man's will determining everything he does.

Your body will respond to your will. Your will passes information to your spirit, to your mind and to your body. When you make a decision of your will that you are going to walk in the love of God because it is His commandment to you, then it will flood your spirit, your mind and your body. You will begin walking in the light as He is in the light.

The Determination of Love

A man who will walk in the absolute life of God, the love of God, and allow that life to flow out of him is unbeatable. Men and women, throughout the Word of God, have done things they couldn't do any other way, but because of the power of God's love, they did it.

A close friend of mine shared this testimony with me, and I would like to share it with you. He and his son were working together. They were driving a little tractor and pulling a log behind it. The log got caught on something and the tractor flipped over on its back. While trying to free his son, both of them got pinned underneath. He quickly crawled out around one side, and suddenly the tractor burst into flames with his son still trapped underneath. He ran around to the back of it and grabbed the fender of the tractor and tried his best to lift it, but with no success. He stopped. Then he said, "All right God, if You've ever helped me, You're going to help me now!" He walked to the back of the tractor, grabbed hold of the fender, picked it up, and got his son out.

Had this man not used his will, his son would have burned to death underneath that tractor and God would probably have gotten the blame for it. He exercised his authority as a believer. He made a decision of his will that he was going to get his son out from under that tractor alive. He also decided God was going to give him the power. And He did! Praise God! I want to add to this, that this man is a man of faith every day, not just when there is trouble. He walks in the Word consistently. That is a major key.

You have a God-made, God-breathed, blood-bought will that is completely intact. It is to be used. God bought and paid for your deliverance and your authority in this earth. That man exercised his God-given authority, and the result was the deliverance of his son.

Built Up in Love

The Bible says the Body of Christ is to build *itself* up in love so we will grow up into Him, into the fullness of the stature of Christ, as we speak the Word to one another in love (Ephesians 4:13, 15-16). The New Testament is words

written by Paul, John, James, Jude, Peter, etc., sharing the
light of God. These men were fellowshiping with the people
in those churches—fellow believers. They would send let-
ters to the churches, and the people were ministered to by
the love and faith of those men. When they began to join
together, things began to happen.

In Ephesians 4, the Word says the ministry of the Body
of Christ is to build itself up in love. We are to grow up
into Jesus in all things—unto the full stature of the Son of
God. *"From whom the whole body fitly joined together and
compacted by that which every joint supplieth, according to the
effectual working in the measure of every part, maketh
increase of the body unto the edifying of itself in love"*
(Ephesians 4:16).

This scripture is saying *we* are the parts of the Body. We are
the joints and ligaments that are holding the Body together in
love. That means every time opportunities for disharmony
present themselves, we *must* stop them right away. Any
thought, any deed, any word that cannot be categorized as
love will separate us, rather than pull us together.

Ephesians 4:11-12 states, *"And he gave some, apostles;
and some, prophets; and some, evangelists; and some, pastors
and teachers; for the perfecting of the saints, for the work of the
ministry, for the edifying of the body of Christ."* The Greek text
has no punctuation. It was placed there at the discretion of
the translators. It should read like this: *He gave some apostles*

some prophets some evangelists some pastors some teachers for the perfecting of the saints for the work of the ministry for the edifying of the body of Christ. These gifts have been given to the Body of Christ to perfect it and get it ready for the work of the ministry. That ministry is the edifying of itself in love.

The Body of Christ, as a whole, has a ministry to itself and a ministry to the world. Its ministry to itself is to build itself up in love.

Verses 13-16 say:

Till we all come in the unity of the faith, and of the knowledge of the Son of God, unto a perfect man, unto the measure of the stature of the fulness of Christ. That we henceforth be no more children, tossed to and fro, and carried about with every wind of doctrine, by the sleight of men, and cunning craftiness, whereby they lie in wait to deceive; But speaking the truth in love, may grow up into him in all things, which is the head, even Christ; from whom the whole body fitly joined together and compacted by that which every joint supplieth, according to the effectual working in the measure of every part, maketh increase of the body unto the edifying of itself in love.

Jesus is not holding the Body of Christ together. He has joined us together. Now we build ourselves up in the love of God. Notice the Body is compacted, or held together, by that which every joint supplies.

Every single member of the Body of Christ has a job to do to hold this Body together. We must communicate the life of God, the light of God to one another, feeding and building one another up in the spirit until we grow up into Jesus in all things, unto the full stature of the Lord Jesus Christ.

The ministry of the Body of Christ to the world is found in Philippians 2:13-16: *"Do all things without murmurings and disputings: that ye may be blameless and harmless, the sons of God, without rebuke, in the midst of a crooked and perverse nation, among whom ye shine as lights in the world; holding forth the word of life."*

Understanding Darkened

Ephesians 4:17-18 says:

This I say therefore, and testify in the Lord, that ye henceforth walk not as other Gentiles walk, in the vanity of their mind, having the understanding darkened, being alienated from the life of God through the ignorance that is in them, because of the blindness of their heart.

The rest of Ephesians, (chapters 4, 5, and even part of

chapter 6) tells us what blinds the mind:

> Let all bitterness, and wrath, and anger, and clamour,
> and evil speaking, be put away from you, with all
> malice: and be ye kind one to another, tenderhearted,
> forgiving one another, even as God for Christ's sake
> hath forgiven you (Ephesians 4:31-32).

Lasciviousness is the lack of dignity, the absence of
restraint. The lascivious attitude thinks, *I may forgive, but I
am not ever going to forget, or I am going to be mad if I want to.*
Allowing this to be your attitude is allowing Satan, as an act
of your will, to darken your thinking. When you accept the
darkness, you walk in it. You have tied God's hands. You
are violating the very commandment of God which is to
love one another. When you do that, you are alienating
yourself from the life of God.

Then when a situation demands that you need healing
in your body, there is no life. When you need to know what
to do in a circumstance, there is no light. It is in you, but
you are walking in death. The Word of God you need cannot flow from your spirit up into your mind or out into
your body.

If you are just *trying* to walk in the commandment of
God's love and you are still operating in strife and unforgiveness, it won't work. The Apostle Paul, in ministering to
the church at Corinth, said, *"I have fed you with milk, and not*

with meat: for hitherto ye were not able to bear it, neither yet now are ye able" (1 Corinthians 3:2). There were envyings and strife and divisions among them. Their minds were blinded. They could not receive the meat of the Word even from the great apostle himself.

Strife will darken the mind and darken the spirit. It will cause the very light of God in you to be darkened. Someone said, "I thought that was absolute light: that there is no darkness in it at all." That is absolutely the truth. "I thought God's love is absolute love: that there is no fear in it at all" That is absolutely the truth.

"Then how can it be darkened?" It is very simple. There is no amount of darkness that can overcome lights that are turned on in a room. No matter how dark it gets, it will never completely dispel the light. But if someone turns out the light, darkness is the result. When you choose strife instead of love, by your will you turn the light out. Darkness is the result.

When you make the decision of your will to walk in the light of God, no amount of darkness can penetrate it. It is when you step over into areas of strife, disharmony, unforgiveness, fear, etc., that the light of God leaves and darkness comes crashing in to steal, kill and destroy. The choice is yours. You can choose to walk in the light or you can choose to walk in darkness (strife, unforgiveness, disharmony). God has *"set before you life and death, blessing and cursing: therefore*

[you] *choose life..."* (Deuteronomy 30:19).

Who does the choosing? You do. You choose to receive salvation. You choose to be healed and walk in divine health. You choose to walk in the love of God. When you choose strife instead of love, when you choose fear instead of faith, when you choose death instead of life, the words that come out your mouth violate the life and victory of Jesus Christ of Nazareth. Then God has no choice. The light is turned off, and darkness is the result.

On the other hand, Satan has no legal right to enforce that darkness in your life when you make the decision to repent. Go to your Advocate, Jesus Christ the righteous. He became sin for you that you might be made the righteousness of God in Him (2 Corinthians 5:21). He is your High Priest. As you confess your sin, God is faithful and just to forgive you and cleanse you from all unrighteousness (1 John 1:9). *"And the blood of Jesus Christ his Son cleanseth us from all sin"* (1 John 1:7). The light is turned back on.

Those things must be dealt with in our lives. Galatians 6:8 says if we sow to the flesh, we *will* reap corruption, but if we sow to the Spirit, we *will* reap life. We must repent of anything that stands between us and our receiving the Word of God in its fullness. We must make the commandment of God the quest of our lives.

When you begin to walk in that love, your spirit man will begin to assimilate the forces that you need in your body and your mind, and they *will* come forth and be applied where they are needed.

The life of God, the light of God, is in your spirit. It *will* flow out as you release it in faith. The absolute love of God is being perfected in you as you act on the commandment of that love. God's love coming forth from your spirit being will produce results. When you see someone in strife, you can go to God and say, "Father, in the Name of Jesus, I am asking for Your life, Your power, Your love to flow in the lives of these people. I am asking forgiveness for them. Give me their forgiveness. I receive it now, in Jesus' Name and I thank You for it." Then take it to them. When you do, you will go to them in an anointing that will break the power of that strife, wipe the blinders off of their eyes and they will fall in love with one another again (1 John 5:16).

In our organization, we resist strife like we resist sickness and disease. We absolutely refuse to allow it to operate at Kenneth Copeland Ministries. The way we do it is walking in God's commandment of love. That love will stop strife before it even gets started.

When you stop strife, you stop Satan's attempts to move you off God's Word and His command to you to love. You would be surprised how many problems are closely linked with strife. They are little things that go unrepented of. The big opportunities we take to get into strife are obvious enough that we quickly repent of them.

It is the little everyday things that are not considered socially wrong that we are slower to repent. We don't notice them as readily, so we unconsciously pass them by. Unless you have received the commandment to love as *a commandment,* we will never even notice the cutting, hurting, sinful words and deeds we commit daily.

We ought to be so in love with each other in the Body of Christ that we cannot keep from fellowshiping together. You are going to be surprised when you get to heaven. Some of your brothers and sisters there will be people you didn't think would be there. There is coming a day when you are going to have to put your arms around people you may not have desired to love here on earth. When that time comes, you will be glad to do it. But right now is when you are going to have to learn to love. Right now is when you must walk in the commandment of God's love as an act of obedience and faith.

The love commandment is the very image of God. It is His perfect will for you and for me. If we will begin to walk in the commandments, we will enforce the law of the Spirit of life. It will absolutely drive out the law of sin and death.

Love Will Intercede

It is our responsibility, as the Body of Christ, to take this message of God's love commandment to every person. We will never walk in that love to any depth until we come to the place where we reach out to the sinner, reach out to the crippled, reach out to the blind, and reach out to the weak with the life, light and love of God. In communicating these forces to them, they will be born again and they will be on their way to complete victory. We can never reach out to them in power until we reach out to one another in love!

We must receive the commandment of God's love as exactly what it is—a commandment to the Body of Christ as a whole. We are connected together by the Spirit of God, and we are to fellowship and intermingle with one another by the Word.

When we learn how to walk in love and learn how to pray the prayer of intercession, we will make ourselves available to the Spirit of God. We will get to the point where we will *know* when we need to pray for one another. Then because of our prayers of intercession according to the Word of God, all things will work together for us who love God and are called according to His purpose (Romans 8:26-28). You will know when I need prayer, and I will know when you need prayer.

It is not true that all bad things in the world work together for the good of those who love God. That scripture has been taken out of context and used to rob Christians and deceive them into allowing the works of Satan to run rampant through their lives.

When the Apostle Paul wrote those words to the

church in Rome, he was referring to intercessory prayer. He was talking about the Spirit of God searching the heart, knowing the mind of the spirit of a man, and praying the perfect will of God in his behalf.

A friend of mine (who is a pastor) and I were discussing this. We began to share with one another about this particular scripture, and the Spirit of God came upon me and began to speak through me. He said:

> I didn't mention the devil in that scripture, did I? I didn't say everything the devil is doing is working to the good of those that are called of God. I am talking about the things of the Body of Christ: the Name of Jesus, the weapons of our warfare, the gifts of the Spirit, the Word of God, and all of the powerful things sent into the earth by Jesus to make the Body of Christ strong and victorious. If My people will begin to pray the intercessory prayer for one another and begin to love one another, I will pray the perfect will of God for the saints through them and the things of the Body of Christ will begin to work together for the good of those who love God and are called according to His purpose. Then, the evil things Satan is doing will not work at all.

When we love to the point that we are willing to stand

in a place of intercession, then we allow the Spirit of God to move. Think of thousands in the Body of Christ standing in a position of intercession. The Spirit of God would then have us all moving together. The reason we have not known anymore about this is because we have not been practicing loving one another. We have not been expressing our love toward one another.

The place to begin is at home. *"If we love one another, God dwelleth in us, and his love is perfected in us"* (1 John 4:12). Practice makes perfect. You will never make any progress in the love of God until you begin practicing it. When you first start out, if you stumble and fall, just repent and keep right on practicing. Love is always first to repent. Love never waits to see who is wrong. It quickly asks forgiveness because it is willing to do anything to stop strife or unforgiveness.

The more you learn to walk in God's commandment of love, the more the light of God will flow out of you. *"But if we walk in the light, as he is in the light, we have fellowship one with another, and the blood of Jesus Christ his Son cleanseth us from all sin"* (1 John 1:7).

There is cleansing that takes place. The blood of Jesus Christ cleanses us from all sin. When you are walking in the light of God—in His love—and opportunities present themselves for you to sin, you will not stumble or fall. You will see the darkness. Life will rise up on the inside of you and show you exactly what to do and the right way to go.

The light of God will point it out, and you will know just how to handle the situation. Then the first thing you will ask yourself anytime those opportunities present themselves again is: "What would love do in this situation?"

The only thing that stands between you and all of God's glory in this earth is your commitment to walk in the commandment of His love. It must be the determination of your will to walk in that love, whether anyone else does or not. There is no other way. It is the will of God for you to obey His commandment of love.

> *The only thing that stands between you and all of God's glory in this earth is your commitment to walk in the commandment of His love.*

God's will is His commandment. If it were not His will, He would not have commanded it. Receive it as such, and walk in the fullness of it. This is how you enforce the law of life.

With every action, there is an equal reaction. The more I fall in love with Jesus, the more determined I am to stop Satan and his works. I am willing to go to whatever length is necessary to walk in the power of God's love.

As the Body of Christ, we must be so full of the Word of God that our first words, our first actions, are directly in line with that Word, rather than operating in the natural realm.

When you are operating in the power of God's love, you walk in areas that absolutely make you dangerous to Satan.

He trembles every time you step out in faith. You control his works. You take from him the very spoils he has plundered and taken years to establish. The life, light, and love of God operating in you will destroy his works and leave him totally helpless. When you become determined to walk in the commandment of love, you can be trusted with more and more of God's anointing power. God can trust you with material prosperity more and more when love is your command and way of life. Abundance in this life is determined directly by how you will love when the pressure is on and the going is rough.

> *Abundance in this life is determined directly by how you will love when the pressure is on and the going is rough.*

When you walk in God's love, you are enforcing the law of life. The gift of God is life and that life is Jesus. Walking in love is walking in life. It is time for us as the Body of Christ to fellowship with God in His Word and with one another in His love. Let's take it out of the physical realm where our feelings get in the way and into the realm of the spirit, where we love one another just because God loves us and for no other reason.

Let's move into the miraculous realm of God's love where together, we can operate in the supernatural power of God where His life and His light are flowing in us and through us to meet every need.

Prayer for Salvation and Baptism in the Holy Spirit

Heavenly Father, I come to You in the Name of Jesus. Your Word says, "Whosoever shall call on the name of the Lord shall be saved" (Acts 2:21). I am calling on You. I pray and ask Jesus to come into my heart and be Lord over my life according to Romans 10:9-10: "If thou shalt confess with thy mouth the Lord Jesus, and shalt believe in thine heart that God hath raised him from the dead, thou shalt be saved. For with the heart man believeth unto righteousness; and with the mouth confession is made unto salvation." I do that now. I confess that Jesus is Lord, and I believe in my heart that God raised Him from the dead. I repent of sin. I renounce it. I renounce the devil and everything he stands for. Jesus is my Lord.

I am now reborn! I am a Christian—a child of Almighty God! I am saved! You also said in Your Word, "If ye then, being evil, know how to give good gifts unto your children: HOW MUCH MORE shall your heavenly Father give the Holy Spirit to them that ask him?" (Luke 11:13). I'm also asking You to fill me with the Holy Spirit. Holy Spirit, rise up within me as I praise God. I fully expect to speak with other tongues as You give me the utterance (Acts 2:4). In Jesus' Name. Amen!

Begin to praise God for filling you with the Holy Spirit. Speak those words and syllables you receive—not in your own language, but the language given to you by the Holy Spirit. You have to use your own voice. God will not force you to speak. Don't be concerned with how it sounds. It is a heavenly language!

Continue with the blessing God has given you and pray in the spirit every day.

You are a born-again, Spirit-filled believer. You'll never be the same!

Find a good church that boldly preaches God's Word and obeys it. Become part of a church family who will love and care for you as you love and care for them.

We need to be connected to each other. It increases our strength in God. It's God's plan for us.

Make it a habit to watch VICTORY Channel™ and become a doer of the Word, who is blessed in his doing (James 1:22-25).

About the Author

Kenneth Copeland is co-founder and president of Kenneth Copeland Ministries in Fort Worth, Texas, and best-selling author of books that include *Honor—Walking in Honesty, Truth and Integrity*, and *THE BLESSING of The LORD Makes Rich and He Adds No Sorrow With It*.

Since 1967, Kenneth has been a minister of the gospel of Christ and teacher of God's Word. He is also the artist on award-winning albums such as his Grammy-nominated *Only the Redeemed, In His Presence, He Is Jehovah, Just a Closer Walk* and *Big Band Gospel*. He also co-stars as the character Wichita Slim in the children's adventure videos *The Gunslinger, Covenant Rider* and the movie *The Treasure of Eagle Mountain*, and as Daniel Lyon in the Commander Kellie and the Superkids™ videos *Armor of Light* and *Judgment: The Trial of Commander Kellie*. Kenneth also co-stars as a Hispanic godfather in the 2009 and 2016 movies *The Rally* and *The Rally 2: Breaking the Curse*.

With the help of offices and staff in the United States, Canada, England, Australia, South Africa and Ukraine, Kenneth is fulfilling his vision to boldly preach the uncompromised WORD of God from the top of this world, to the bottom, and all the way around. His ministry reaches millions of people worldwide through daily and Sunday TV broadcasts, magazines, teaching audios and videos, conventions and campaigns, and the World Wide Web.

Learn more about Kenneth Copeland Ministries
by visiting our website at **kcm.org**